D1073888

The Ubiquitous Wench
&
Other Pure and Punny Limericks

John Price

The Ubiquitous Wench
&
Other Pure and Punny Limericks

Published by John Price
2447 Hi River Road
Hiawassee, Georgia 30546
(706) 896-7891
jbprice@alltel.net

ISBN 0-9675416-1-1
Library of Congress
Catalog Card Number: 2002090959

The Ubiquitous Wench
&
Other Pure and Punny Limericks

by
John Price

By the Same Author

Words of Memory (Poetry)
Stompin' at the Senior Center (Light Verse)
The Price Papers (Non-Fiction)*
The Gowks of County Lee (Fiction)*

*In search of a publisher

Preface

The origin of the limerick is not definitely known, but Langford Reed, in his *The Complete Limerick Book,* advances the theory that it is an old French form of verse brought back to Limerick, Ireland, by the returning veterans of the Irish Brigade, which served in France from 1691 to about 1780. Its officers may have imported the form to Limerick in Ireland, whence the name of the form. Alternatively, the name may derive from the carousers' refrain "Will you come up to Limerick?" This refrain was once sung in chorus by the assembled drunkards after one among them had sung an impromptu solo verse telling his adventures. The solo need not have been a limerick as we know it. Perhaps it was sung to a roughly similar form. Perhaps it was even common at one time to sing limericks. Or perhaps not.

Or perhaps the entire theory promoted by Mr. Reed is askew, for limericks can be found in manuscripts many centuries old. One example is in the British museum's Harleian Manuscript of 1322:

> The lion is wondirliche strong,
> & ful of wiles of wo;
> > & wether he pleye
> > other take his preye
> he can not do bot slo (slay).

The 17th and 18th centuries give a glimpse of the limerick's early potential—the one we all heard as children, "Hickory, Dickory, Dock," dates from 1744—but, unlike the innocence of that verse, satire and the erotic themes in many drinking songs of that period were the rule. With all its comings and goings, it was the 19th century that saw the limerick finally established in the celebrated form that you see in this book. Edward Lear (1812-1888) is generally credited with the popularization of the limerick via his *Book of Nonsense* published in 1846, but, in fact, two important collections were published before that, both anonymous and both known to Lear. *The History of Sixteen Wonderful Old Women* and *Anecdotes of Fifteen Gentlemen* were published in 1821 and 1822 by John Marshal of London. Lear, though, never claimed to have invented the limerick. He wrote that he discovered in it a "form of verse lending itself to limitless varieties for rhymes and pictures...." (I, too, believe that limericks are more effective when accompanied by illustrations, but—alas!—I cannot claim the origination of those depicted herein as could Mr. Lear, who was an artist.) With its popularity came parodies by famous poets of the time, notable among them Swinburne and Rossetti.

Following the gentle beginnings of Lear's wildly nonsensical verse came an aversion to the obscene and indecent limericks predominating today. Some people thought (and think!) that to work properly, the limerick must be pornographic, sexist, racist, or otherwise offensive for the last line to impact. I think differently. Risque? Okay! But limericks akin to the "humor" of Eddie Murphy, Whoopi Goldberg, George Carlin, Kevin James, and others of the shock culture who perform "in concert" are not funny. One of the sad days of my years was when I recently bought a book of limericks written by the world-famous author, Isaac Asimov, and his friend, the equally famous poet, John Ciardi. Both, now deceased, were heroes of mine. While I still admire their serious writings, they have fallen from the respect-crafted pedestals they once occupied in my mind.

The limerick is a story in five lines of verse. While the usual presentation of the limerick has the third and fourth lines indented, the overall visual arrangement can vary, as it does in this book. What are *not* discretionary—if, that is, one is to be true to the form—are the meter and rhyme scheme. In respect of meter, the first, second, and fifth lines usually consist of nine beats while lines three and four are customarily of six beats. The third, sixth, and ninth beats of lines one, two, and five are accentuated; the third and sixth beats of lines three and four are also accentuated. This metrical pattern—two short syllables and a long—is called "anapestic." As concerns rhyme, the first, second, and fifth lines must rhyme. The third and fourth lines must also rhyme, but the rhyme must be different from that of the other three lines.

Limericks derive from many sources. Puns are an excellent source for the creation of limericks, and a good measure of limericks from that source constitute this offering. Other sources are historical and contemporary quotations by well-known people, the misadventures of prominent personalities, humorous stories and jokes, and unintended misprints in published articles. The title of this book is born of the last of such sources.

I really, *really* hope you enjoy this book. Limericks can easily become addictive. Like potato chips, "just one more" may overtake you. Many famous intellectuals and serious poets found them so consuming that they spent a part of their writing careers in producing them: Oliver Wendell Holmes, W.H. Auden, Lord Tennyson, Rudyard Kipling, Robert Louis Stevenson, and W.S. Gilbert of Gilbert & Sullivan comic opera fame were some of them. So, if you're fond of limericks, you may wish, as they did, to try your hand. Jest for the pun of it.

John Price
Hiawassee, Georgia
April, 2002

Dedication

To my sons, their mates, and my grandchildren

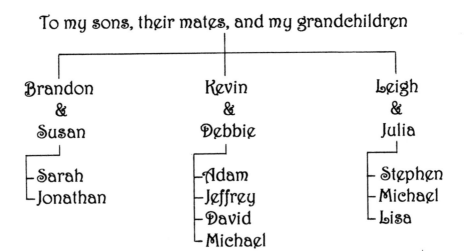

Brandon	Kevin	Leigh
&	&	&
Susan	Debbie	Julia

- Sarah
- Jonathan

- Adam
- Jeffrey
- David
- Michael

- Stephen
- Michael
- Lisa

The Ubiquitous Wench
And Other Pure & Punny Limericks

Contents

Preface

Dedication

Warning!

The Ubiquitous Wench
And Other Pure & Punny Llimericks

Contents

The Ubiquitous Wench
And Other Pure & Punny Limericks

Contents

The Ubiquitous Wench
And Other Pure & Punny Limericks

Contents

Acknowledgments

<u>Warning!</u>

Limericks are addictive and, thus, may be hazardous to your health, causing spasms of unrestrained guffaw, chronic chuckling, and permanent laugh-lines around the eyes. Should these or like symptons occur, put the book down and call, e-mail, or write me (see the copyright page) for remedial advice.

John Price

HIAWASSEE (The Towns Sentinel), December 6, 2000 - Sheriff Rudy Eller...released information last week concerning the apprehension of those involved in bashing down at least ten mailboxes...the owner of the vehicle (used in the bashing) admitted using his car to take down the mailboxes. Apparently the wench (sic) on the front of the 4x4 '87 Chevy Blazer....

The Ubiquitous Wench

I've seen wenches in many odd places,
Such as birthday cakes and genies' vases,
But to see one append
To a Chevy's front end
Is a site which all others erases.*

* Although it's probably a good place to unwind.

Admission

I've always been one who concurred
That children are best seen, not heard.
But what with the way
The kids dress today,
I would freely admit I have erred.

Poem on the Range

Two tourists were viewing a herd of plains buffalo. One said, "These are the mangiest, scroungiest, most moth-eaten critters I ever did see." To which the other, stopping in front of a pair of the beasts, replied:

"And these are the worst of the herd!"
A statement the pair overheard.
Said the one, name of Roy,
To his bison bro, "Boy,
Talk about your discouraging word!"

Good News; Bad News

The TV man, looking dismayed,
Said, submitting his bill to be paid,
"Your tube is all right,
But the cabinet's a fright.
It has Dutch elm disease, I'm afraid."

COPENHAGEN (Reuters), April 9, 1999 - Women serving in the Danish army are furious over the military's purchase—handled by a male officer—of the same size brassieres for 500 women soldiers. "They have bought one model only and think that it can fit all of us. But we are big and small, thick and thin," Lance Corporal Ulla Bekker Madsen said in the tabloid Ekstra-Bladet Friday.

Major O.P. Soerensen, the procurement officer responsible for the purchase, told the paper that an order had been placed for C-cup size 100 brassieres, which the manufacturer said fitted 90 percent of Danish women.

The Copenhagen C-Cup Caper
or
Something is Rotten in Denmark

In the Danes' army once there was living
A major with major misgivings.
'Twas a major mistake
That this major did make,
And the ladies weren't ones for forgiving.

Seems the major placed large purchase orders
For brassieres that he shouldn't have orter:
He bought "one size fits all,"
Neither big, neither small.
Last seen, he was crossing the border.

Parsimony Incarnate

Widow Quayle went to the local newspaper office to submit the obituary for her recently deceased husband. The obit editor informed her of a charge of fifty cents per word. The thrifty Mrs. Quayle paused—reflected—and said, "Well, then, let it read: Fred Quayle died."

Said the editor, sifting his mail,
"Seven words is the min, Mrs. Quayle."
Widow Quayle's brow knit
As she chewed on her bit.
"All right, then, add: Golf clubs for sale."

Que?

It is many odd phrases I've seen;
Some gracious, some cutting, some 'tween.
But the one I like soul-ly
Is *Como frijoles?*
It's Spanish for "How have you bean?"

Brown Paper Navarre

"Anyone seen Brown Paper Navarre?"
Sheriff Boone asked the boys at the bar.
    "What's he look like?" asked one
    Of the sons-of-a-gun.
"Waal," the sheriff drawled through his cigar,

"He wears brown paper pants and a hat,
And a brown paper waistcoat, at that.
    And his shirt's paper, too—
    As are both of his shoes—
And he sports a brown paper cravat."

A murmur coursed through the saloon
Like the repeating cry of the loon.
    And then one buckaroo
    Asked in time with his chew,
"What's he wanted for?" "Rustlin'," says Boone.

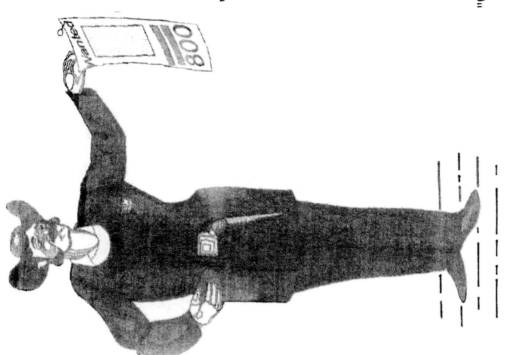

8

N ot everything about the flood
is in the bible:

Noah Can Do

"Go forth," Noah said. "Multiply."
Two snakes said they couldn't comply.
"And why not?" Noah gasped.
"We can't," said the asps,
"Because we are adders. That's why!"

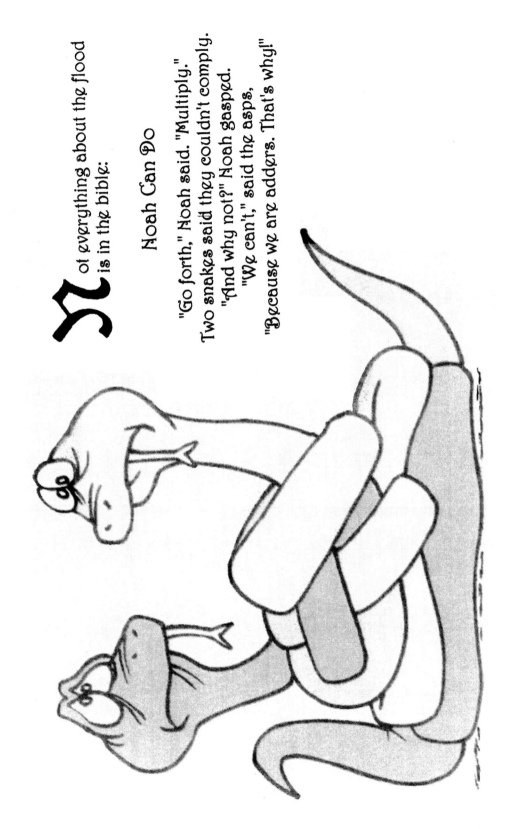

Is This a Great Country— or What!

Yakov Smirof,
from Russia of late,
was asked
if he'd yet picked a date
for his wedding to be.
"I can *bring* date,"
cried he.
"Don't tell *me*
this country
she not great!"

Quirkish Turkish

A Turkish mosque once I saw bore
A sign reading "Don't Salaam the Door."
Which reminds me a tad,
A salaam that's gone bad
Is a false salaam forevermore.

It Could Happen to Anyone

Identical twins, Joe and Jake,
Lived together on Woebegone Lake.
Suicidal, they say,
Joey lost it one day
And killed his twin, Jake, by mistake.

Run, Don't Walk

In the cockroaches' world, liaison
Means the girls mate just once, whereupon
It is pregnant they be
For life. Now you see
Why they run when the light is turned on!

ver since General MacArthur delivered his famous "Old soldiers never die" speech, there has been a rash of quotations akin to the one in that speech about other professions.

Old Bankers

Old bankers, 'tis said, never die;
And 'tis furthermore said they don't lie.
Thus, I have to believe
What one once said to me:
"We merely lose interest," he sighed.

Navratilova's Trepidation

When Martina's defection was near,
It was not without some sense of fear.
"Ere I give them the slip,"
Marti asked on the ship,
"Are you positive Czechs are cached here?"

Chipper, 1; Coach, 0

The frustrated coach tore his hair
When the Chipper continued to err.
He asked what it could be:
Ignorance? Apathy?
"I don't know," said the lad, "and don't care!"

How Come?

I bought me a dog deaf and dumb,
An' his sight, too, long since had succumbed.
When Lolita de Smollett
Asked what I would call it,
"'Tain't no matter," I said, "he won't come."

Such a Problem!

Steven Wright has a physical plight
That he hates with a passionate might.
   "When my foot falls asleep
   In the daytime," Steve weeps,
   "That means it will be up all night!"

18

Long before Harry Potter, there was Tom Swift. Some ninety-seven juvenile books in four series beginning in 1910 were published. Still popular today are "Tom Swiftys," verbal puns which were the spawn of the series.

I first heard Tom Swiftys from Mom,
Who expressed them with nary a qualm.
One I'll never forget
Is this verbal vignette:
"I detest milking cows," uttered Tom.

Just for Luck

I was strolling in London's Piccadilly Circus on a fall evening in 1945 when this lady, in a Marlene-like voice, whispered:

"Would you fancy to sleep with me, ducks,
For a tener? C'mon, just for luck!"
"I'm really not tired,"
I said, uninspired,
"But I surely could use fifty bucks!"

An Eskimo No-No

Two Eskimos, cold as a sheet, lit
A fire in their boat. Can you beat it?
The boat sank, proving true
The old maxim that you
Cannot have your kayak and heat it!

A Birthday Wish
for an Olde Friend

There is a good neighbor named Ben
Who in years is now seven times ten.
Men as old number few,
And of those—sad but true—
Most are dead! Happy Birthday, olde friend.

Lad

Gustav Jones had a collie named Lad
Whom he loved with a love ironclad.
Then one day Mom told Gus
Lad was hit by a bus
And had gone up to Heaven, he had.

To her wonder, Gus merely said "Aw!"
And went out with his bat and his ball.
On return, he asked, "Say,
Where is Laddie today?
He's not hearkened at all to my call."

Mrs. Jones thought her son had gone mad.
"But I told you, dear, God's taken Lad."
The boy's eyes became blear
Ere he burst into tears.
"I thought," Gustav wailed, "you said 'Dad'!"

23

Eh?

Walking two miles a day, the doc vowed,
Would Jacques' health and fine fettle endow.
One month passed and the doc
Got a phone call from Jacques:
"I'm in Boston. What should I do now?"

The Gratuity

When the dowager, cold as a stone,
Left a tip of minutia unknown,
The waiter turned green.
"This must be what they mean
By the tip of the iceberg!" he groaned.

Applesauce

The story that evil is found
In a fruit on a tree ain't too sound.
The more plausible cause
To my mind is it was
The tomato that lay on the ground.

Lincoln's Law

No one in his right mind would dispute
Honest Abe in his day was a "hoot."
He once said his advice is
That folks with no vices
Have very few virtues, to boot!

Good or Bad?

In the fight with Saddam, we employed
Both the genders; that is, girl and boy.
      'Tis said that the mix
      Of the studs and the chicks
      Created a sexual alloy

In two-thirds of the units we had
Which, in numbers, is more than a tad.
      Morale was affected
      The army detected.
      It didn't say if good or bad!

The Three-Wood Holocaust

Once there was a golfer name of Morgan Robertson whose drive landed on an anthill. Rather than move the ball, Morgan decided to hit it where it lay. He gave a mighty swing. Clouds of dirt and sand and ants exploded from the spot—alas! everything but the golf ball. It sat in the same spot. So Morgan lined up and tried another shot. Dirt, sand, and ants went flying again. The golf ball didn't even wiggle. Two ants survived.

"Oh, my God!" cried one ant, "what do y'all
Think that we ought to do, Jimmie Paul?"
      "Well, now, sweet Bonnie Sue,
      I don't know about *you*,
      But *I'm* going to get on the ball!"

The Truth, Forsooth

Now, auctioneers long in the tooth
Don't die. That's the absolute truth.
It's been fathomed as fact
As far back as time's tracked
That they just look forbidding—forsooth!

A Change of Menu

"My view of life suddenly shifted
When I realized that I was gifted
In behavior risque,"
Mae West told me one day.
"Yes, I once was Snow White—but I drifted!"

Sho 'Nuff

A socialite
in Washington
once sniffed
to my friend,
Billy Don:
"Breeding's
everything—
right?"
Replied Billy,
eyes bright:
"Ah cain't say,
but
Ah shore know
it's fun!"

Is There a Difference?

There was an old man from Dundee
Who, in person, addressed Sam MacKee.
When told Sam was dead,
"Please forgive me," he said.
"I thought he was British, you see!"

The Real Hannibal

Asked the cannibal's wife, Marguerite, "Oh,
How come you aren't eating, Philippeo?"
"I don't know," sighed her mate,
"Why I've languished of late.
I guess I'm just fed up with people."

Gloria's Euphoria

It was Gloria Steinem who vowed
She would never get married—nohow!
When asked why, Steinem said,
With a toss of her head,
"I can't mate in captivity. Ciao!"

Wee Jenny's Plaint

Asked Wee Jenny one night with a sigh,
"Daddy dear, I'm so tired I could cry.
Do my homework tonight?"
"Dear, it wouldn't be right."
"Oh, I know that. But give it a try!"

leaning out the aviary at a run-down zoo, Ben, the keeper, found two finches that had died of old age. He picked them up and placed them in a sack. After cleaning the cage, he put the sack in his cart and moved on to the primate cage, where he found two elderly chimps had also died of natural causes. "Waste not, want not," philosophized Ben as he put the chimps in the sack with the birds.

Better than Berries

At feeding time, zoo keeper Ben
Placed the sack in the grizzly bear's den.
With a look of disdain
The grizzly complained,
"Holy smokes: finch and chimps. Not again!"

Joe's Dictum

Asked the seamstress with innate foresight,
"Cut your pants long or short? What is right?"
    "Well, I really don't know,"
    Said the weatherman, Joe.
"Tell you what: Cut them just fair-in-height."

Good Question, Son

A mother and baby camel are talking. The baby camel asks, "Mom, why have I got these huge tree-toed feet?" The mother says, "As you trek across the desert, those feet will help you to stay on top of the soft, soft sand." The young camel then asks, "Mom, why have I got these long, long eyelashes?" "To keep the sand out of your eyes on the long, long trips through the endless desert," says the mother. "And, Mom, why have I got these great big huge humps on my back?" asks the young one. "They are there to help you store precious water for your long, long treks across the desert so you can go without drinking for long, long periods," answers the mother. "So, let me understand this," says the lad:

"I have huge feet, the better to stand,
And eyelashes to cope with the sand.
And these humps on my back
Store the water I'll lack
On a long trip across Arab land."

"That's right," says his mother. "Do you
Have more questions you'd like to pursue?"
"Yes, I have," says her son.
"There is only just one:
Why the heck am I here in the zoo?"

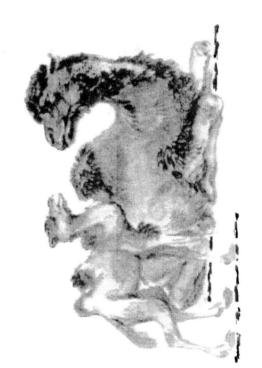

39

Electronic Gall

Computers are smart, all in all,
But mine has the human touch: gall.
When the chip by Intel
Makes a slip nonpareil,
It blames it on one down the hall!

Don't Matter

In the space noted SEX, Sally Donne
Wrote "Yes, twice a day, not just one."
"We mean 'male' or 'female'?"
Said the clerk, Mr. Dale.
"Oh, it don't," said Ms. Donne, "matter none!"

No Rock Jock Am I

Though the Lord knows I really have tried,
I cannot seem to grow things outside.
My rock garden, now,
Shouldn't take much know-how,
Yet, last week it was, three of them died!

Take Heed: Accede

A Wizard worked in a factory. Everything was fine except that certain miscreants, taking advantage of his good nature, would steal his parking spot. This continued until he put up the following sign:

"To the Wizard this space is bestowed.
To all others misfortune will bode.
What this means, wizard-wise,
Is that henceforth you guys
Who elect to park here will be toad."

A Time to Wonder

Many people
since Time
early dawned
believe miracles are
the Lord's spawn
without even a
blink
of a moment
to think
what He's saving
up
for later on!

VERMONT (Associated Press), June 19, 1998 - A Vermont college student undressed in the middle of a dance at the senior prom.

Who Does, Then?

There was a young lady from Stowe
Who disrobed at the senior prom. Whoa!
Said the school's president,
"She does not represent
The fine student body *I* know."

Florida

Though Florida reeks sun and sand,
It reeks, too, as the home of the scam.
But my realtor, Hughes,
Wired me wonderful news:
On my property there they found land!

I'll Say!

"A four-wood and putter are what
I need for *this* hole," bragged Phil Mutt.
Phil's shot went ten feet.
His caddy, Frank Peet,
Said, "And now for one hell of a putt!"

Everybody knows of the Wright brothers and their historic flight at Kitty Hawk in 1903. But few know of the conversation which immediately followed:

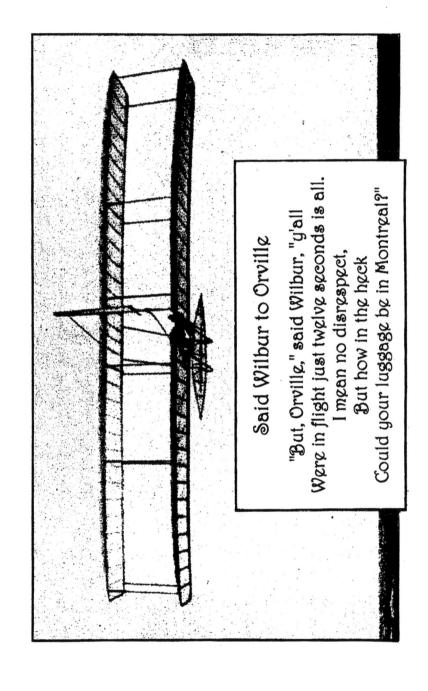

Said Wilbur to Orville

"But, Orville," said Wilbur, "y'all
Were in flight just twelve seconds is all.
I mean no disrespect,
But how in the heck
Could your luggage be in Montreal?"

Not Until, Little Joe

In his history class, Little Joe
Raised his hand: "I would sure like to know,"
Said he, "when I'll learn
All about Clinton's term."
"When you're twenty-one," said Mrs. Stowe.

49

The
Dangerfield
Incentive

"The time
I was
kidnapped,"
Rod cracked,
"The ransom note
took
a grim tack:
'We want
seventy grand.
Unmarked bills.
Understand?
Or else
you will
get your kid back!'"

Red Reverend Redding

When the lady's name from mem'ry fled,
Reverend Redding's face bloomed a bright red.
"Ma'am, I feel so ashamed
I can't think of your name,
But your faith is familiar," he said.

Bug Off, Antony!

Cleopatra said "No" and just smiled
When Marc posed that they walk down the aisle.
Asked why, she howled, "Hey,
I ain't gonna. No way!
Don't you know I'm the queen of denial?"

Odd Odds

There is on a farm in Belgrade
A chicken who's treated like God.
It swallowed, one morn,
A horse racing form
And, instead of eggs, now it lays odds.

How Accommodating Can You Get?

After a thirty-day whirlwind romance, Seth and Fay, though knowing next-to-nothing about each other, got married. After the honeymoon, Seth confessed he was a golf addict:

"Though it seems I'm of caring bereft,
I must play every day," proclaimed Seth.
"I'm out, too, every day;
I'm a hooker," 'fessed Fay.
"Okay, Fay. We'll just play doglegs left!"

Hey, He's from Texas!

In the early part of 2001, China's Premier Zhu Rongji paid a state visit to the U.S. Here's how reporters reacted at the press conference:

When the president, George Number Two,
Introduced to the press Premier Zhu,
Despite English quite grim,
They were patient with him—
And polite to the Chinese guy, too!

Bill's Will

There was a bold lawyer named Bill
Whose tenacity equalled his skill.
Bill once stayed up all night
In a tireless fight
To try to break Widow Jones' will.

An Alliteratively Orthographical Adventure in Vocabularyland

Carly Crawford's a crossword fanatic,
One who favors a mood monocratic.
It is certainly sure
When she dies she'll inter
Six feet down, three across in quadratic.

All Hail the Snail

"I will purchase your car *quid pro quo*,"
Said the snail, "on condition you'll show
A big 'S' on the door
So when past folks I roar
They'll exclaim, 'Look at that "S" car go!'"

To the Reader: I Need Your Help

Hi,

I have a small favor to ask. I have friends from Pakistan who are camping their way around the States. They are ready to leave here and they have asked me if I know where they might be able to go without spending large amounts of money. I said I would try my friends and family for accommodations.

They travel light and bring all their own camping gear and only require a small place to set up. Anyway, I have given them your name and address, anticipating that you won't mind. I've attached a picture to help with identification in case they turn up.

Thanks for understanding.

60

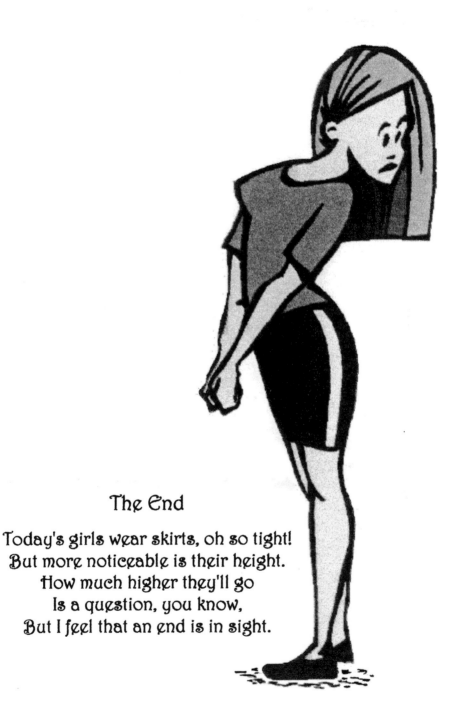

The End

Today's girls wear skirts, oh so tight!
But more noticeable is their height.
How much higher they'll go
Is a question, you know,
But I feel that an end is in sight.

Whistler's Mother

One night at Hotel Knickerbocker,
James Whistler was met with a shocker:
Gaily dancing a samba
Was Jimmy's old mama.
Said her son, "Have you gone off your rocker!"

Oh, Good!

A man I once knew, name of Sam,
Went to get a full fiscal exam.
When he'd finished, Doc said,
With a shake of his head,
"Alas, Sam, I've news good and bad.

"You've just three months to live to the end.
Sorry, Sam. That's the bad news, my friend."
"And the good?" Samuel said
With a hang of his head.
"Your cholesterol's only one-ten."

Wholly Unholy

"Woe is me!" bemoaned Earl to the priest.
"I have surely been bit by the Beast.
I just learned—oy, vey!—
That my brother is gay;
And the pity is, that is the least

"Of my sorrow, my shame, and my strife:
My son, too, I found, lives that life."
"Is there no one home, Earl,
Who gives women a whirl?"
Asked the priest. "Yeah," said Earl, "my wife."

Near Unanimous

"A vasectomy?" queried Doc Pew.
"That's a major decision. Have you
Talked it out with your family?"
"Oh, yes," said Fred Manly.
"They favor it—fifteen to two!"

Love Defined

Definitions of love never cease.
Most are platitudes steeped in caprice.
But the one I like most
Is this little riposte:
Love's composed of two sins: war and peace.

Skunks, Too?

That religion's for humans is true;
It is less known that skunks indulge, too.
That God gave them their due
Is borne out by the clue
That He gave them their very own pew.

Trader Phyfe

"I got," said the first golfer, Phyfe,
"A good set of clubs for my wife."
Golfer Two, name of Lee,
Said, "For sure, that must be
The best trade you've made in your life!"

Thor

Thor, a principal god in Norse mythology was, after Odin, the most powerful; to wit, he almost conquered Elli (old age) in a wrestling match. But he didn't and, like us mortals, grew old. Along the way he, as mortals are also inclined, lost some of youth's amenities. Like memory, for instance.

"I am *Thor*," Thor the Thunder God shrilly
Proclaimed as he spurred on his filly.
"You alone are to blame,"
Neighed the horse, name of Mame:
"You forgot to thaddle me, thilly!"

Of Course Not!

The claims man informed Mr. Brown
His policy covered, he'd found,
The fall from the roof—
Of that he had proof—
But it didn't for hitting the ground!

What Else!

Ms. Hillary Clinton spent hours
Developing Slick Willy's powers.
Thus, she got really miffed
When she bought him a gift
And he said that he'd rather have Flowers.

Meta-Limericks

meta-limerick is a poetic verse that "plays" with or comments on the limerick form but is not a true limerick because it doesn't "scan"; i.e., doesn't precisely follow the metrical pattern, rhyme scheme, or stanzaic form (or all three) of the true limerick. Here is an example by one Elliott Moreton:

A cardiac patient named Fred
Made a limerick up in his head.
But before he had time
To write down the last line

And another by Anonymous:

There was a young man from Peru
Whose limericks stopped at line two

Aristotle Who?

Aristotle once said at Parnassus,
"If the planet were empty of lasses,
All the toys that wealth brings
Wouldn't mean a darn thing."
Not the first Aristotle. Onassis!

Okay, But Don't Fall Over

I did drugs as a youth of the past,
But now that I'm old I have cast
Them aside. What the heck!
I can get their effect
By just standing up now really fast!

The Game

"I stayed up," bleary-eyed Steven Wright
Said to me, "playing poker all night.
And though stud was the name
What it really became
Was a game that turned into a fright!"

"And why was that so? Please confide
In me, Steven, old buddy," I pried.
"Well, I played tarot cards
With results quite bizarre:
A full house and four people died!"

Right On, Phyl

Phyllis Diller once said,
"Wives, unite!
Should your mate and you
argue at night,
don't fall for that jive
marriage gurus contrive:
'Never go to bed mad.'
Stay and fight!"

Everybody Knows

Everybody knows you can't catch a leprechaun. Everybody, that is, except the golfer on an Irish course who one day hit his drive off the tenth tee into the woods. Finding the ball, the golfer also found a very little man with a very big bump on his head lying unconscious next to it. Upon being massaged into consciousness, the little man said to the golfer, "I'm a leprechaun. Since you are the first to catch me, I will grant you three wishes." The golfer politely refused the offer and walked away. "Well," said the leprechaun to himself, "as everybody knows, I'm obliged to do something for him. I'll give him those things that all golfers want: unlimited funds, a great golf game, and a fantastic sex life.

A year later, the golfer, playing the same tenth hole, hits a fairway shot into the same woods in which his errant tee shot was hit the year prior. And, coincidence that it may seem, he comes across the same leprechaun. "How are you?" the man asks. "I'm fine," replies the leprechaun, "and how, may I ask, is your golf game?" "Just great!" says the golfer. "I'm under par every round." "I did that for you," says the leprechaun. "And how is your money holding out?" "It's absolutely incredible!" exclaims the golfer. "Every time I reach into my pocket—every single time!—I find a hundred-pound note." "I did that for you, too," smiles the leprechaun. "And your sex life; how's that?" The golfer looks at the leprechaun sheepishly. "Well," he replies, "maybe once or twice a week."

"Once or twice!" says the elf with a whine. "Don't you think that is rather benign?"
Says the golfer, "Now, cease! That's not bad for a priest with a parish as little as mine!"

77

Don't Call Her Madam, Either

"When you talk to our neighbors, just say
That your mother delights in crochet,"
Said his dad to young Dan.
"That is much better than
'Mom's a cool happy hooker.' Okay?"

Rita Rudner had a problem:

Some Friends!

"As a child, I'd no sister or brother,
No one to converse with but Mother.
To serve fantasy's ends
I imagined two friends.
But they only would talk to each other!"

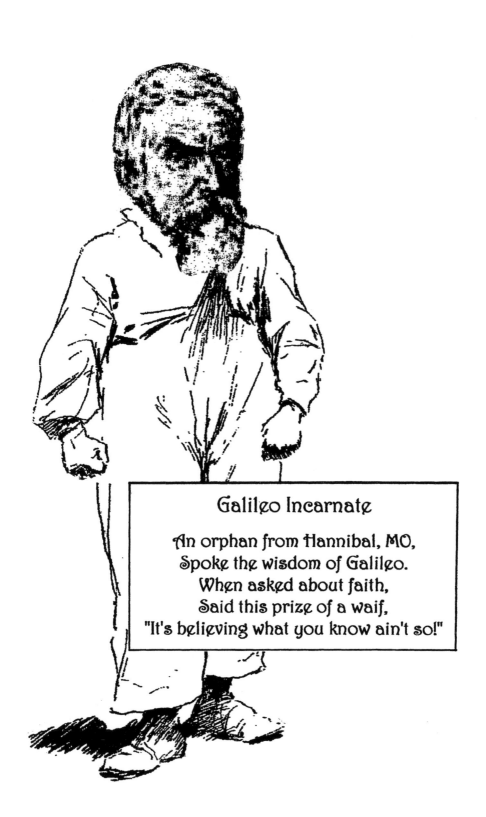

Galileo Incarnate

An orphan from Hannibal, MO,
Spoke the wisdom of Galileo.
When asked about faith,
Said this prize of a waif,
"It's believing what you know ain't so!"

Wright, Steve!

"Last night, in a period of futz,
I played a blank tape, like a klutz.
In the room next to mine
Dwells a bonafide mime.
He went utterly fluttery nuts!"

So What Else is New?

As the issue grew somewhat in doubt,
The senators started to shout.
"You're lying!" cried Hyde,
To which Hollings replied,
"I *know* that. But just hear me out!"

Zsa Zsa's Firey Advice
Concerning the Candle-Like Nature of Man

It is many a mate she's befriended,
Has Zsa Zsa Gabor, who extended
This piece of advice
About husbands to wives:
"They go out if they're left unattended."

Whoa! Here Come the Letters!

I'd vote for the house cat's disjunction
With less than a little compunction.
Their purpose, it's plain,
Is to help us explain
That not all things in nature have function.

Cicero's Complaint

There was an old goat, Cicero,
Who ate film just as if *comme il faut*,
And then after, complain
That the script was innane:
"The book was much better, you know!"

On Second Thought

I was strolling down Main Street in Hiawassee when I found a wallet containing two hundred dollars. My first thought was to keep it rather than return it, but....

Then I pondered an inward confession:
How would I feel if I'd lost possession
    Of a sum such as that?
    And I knew then—out flat—
I'd have wanted to be taught a lesson!

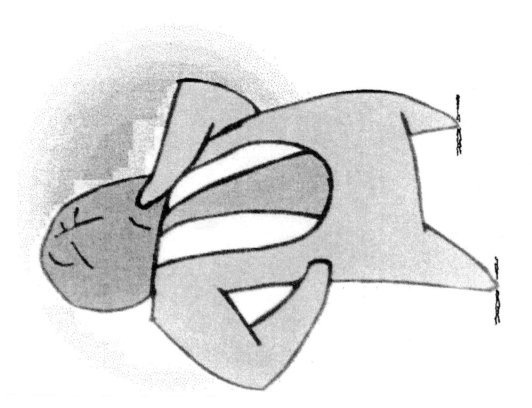

No Need for a Course, of Course

Lou has been stranded on a desert island for ten years. One day, a woman is washed ashore clutching a waterproof bag she has been using as a life preserver. After she dries off and they are talking comfortably around a little fire, the woman, name of Sue, smiles, "I don't suppose you smoked before you were stranded here, did you?" she asks. "Why, yes, I did," says Lou. Sue produces two cigarettes from her bag and they puff contentedly for awhile. "I don't suppose you drank before you were stranded, did you?" Sue asks. "Yes, I did," responds Lou. Sue produces a flask of fine brandy from her bag and they drink. As they are finishing their drinks, Sue says, "So, you've been on this island for ten years...without a woman, huh?" Lou replies, "That's true!"

"Don't suppose," Susan drawls with this cue, "you would hanker to play around, Lou."

With a look of surprise in his eyes Lou replies, "You've golf clubs in that duffel bag, too?"

87

Rodney's Complaint

Rodney Dangerfield gets no respect—
Not a speckle, a freckle, a fleck.
A bazaar belly dancer,
When he tried to romance her,
Told him he turned her stomach. Oy, yech!

A Saint He Ain't

Saint Augustine was a coquet
Who lived life in a state of regret.
In his earlier day
He was oft heard to pray,
"Lord, help me be pure—but not yet!"

Syntactical Wisdom

Steven Wright, in a past interview,
Scored with this philosophical coup:
If the sentence, "I am,"
Is the shortest for man,
Can the longest be counted, "I do"?

A statue of Franklin D. Roosevelt in a wheelchair was unveiled a time back. Acknowledging the former president's disability may set a trend for presidential statuary.

A Plea for Me and Humanity

Franklin D. in a wheelchair's fine,
But don't sculp Willy Clinton behind
His desk. Don't you see,
That would end it for me:
Off to Mexico I'd be inclined.

Point of View

A dandelion farmer named Moe
Found a tulip in one of his rows.
In a bit of a snit
Moe gave it a rip
Saying, "Weeds are a pain, don't you know!"

Next?

The psychiatrist, Dr. T. Rex,
Probed Roberto, who seemed rather vexed.
"What's your problem?" asked T.
"No one listens to me,"
Said Roberto. The doctor said, "Next?"

Albert's Surprise

"I reduced," said the VP, Al Gore,
"Federal payrolls by thousands—and more!"
Which, to Albert's surprise,
Has occasioned a rise
In the welfare and unemployed poor.

Rest in Peace

A flasher named Ewing is being helped by his psychiatrist. She is hypnotizing him into believing that his organ has died. When she is finished, Ewing leaps from the couch and throws open his coat.

"Wha...what," said the doc, "are you doing?
I told you it's *dead*, Mr. Ewing!"
But Ewing the while
Wore a penile smile.
Crowed the flasher: "Today is the viewing!"

I'll Bet!

Three men are in a hunting lodge sitting around a log fire with their dogs. The first man says, "Mah dawg's name is Woodworker. Go, Woodworker!" The dog grabs a piece of wood and, with his teeth and paws, fashions a beautiful figuring. The next man says, "Mah dawg is called Stoneworker. Go, Stoneworker!" The dog drags a rock from the hearth and gnaws a fantastic carving. Says the third fellow of his dog:

"Mah dawg, Ironworker, fer shore,
Makes yore dawgs look pitiful poor.
If Ah far these tongs here,
Touch him once on the rear,
Watch him fast make a bolt fer the door!"

No Wiser Words

Said the wisest of men,
Old King Saul,
"The truth of the matter,
y'all,
is one robin won't bring
the beginning of spring,
BUT
one lark often signals
a fall!"

97

Zsa Zsa the Housekeeper

"As a housekeeper, I am the best,"
Said Zsa Zsa one night to her guest.
"Every time I divorce
I make certain, of course,
That I keep the man's house—nothing less!"

East is East and West is West

Of all of the countries frequented,
The one where I felt less contented
And, sadly, withdrawn
Was the isle of Taiwan.
I just never could get oriented.

Good Question!

The cop addressed Debbie Ann Burr,
Who'd been driving at eighty-nine per:
"Ma'am, please give me your name."
Replied Debbie, aflame,
"And how *then* shall I be known, sir?"

Acknowledgments

Frequently, jokes and funny stories become part of folklore, and no one knows who first told them. Although all of the limericks in this book are original, many of them are based on humorous sayings or stories from secondary sources. I have, in such instances, given credit—often in the limerick itself—where possible. Tracing was sometimes difficult, and I apologize if I missed anyone.

The history of limericks recounted in the preface is based on the following sources:

- Isaac Asimov & John Ciardi, *Limericks* (New York: Gramercy Books, 2000) pp. v-vi.
- William Flint Thrall & Addison Hibbard, *A Handbook to Literature* (New York: Odyssey Press, 1936) pp. 227-228.
- Alex Preminger & T.V.F. Brogan, editors, *The New Princeton Encyclopedia of Poetry and Poetics* (New York: MJF Books, 1993) pp. 693-694.
- Linda Marsh, editor, *Limericks for All Occasions* (New York: Welcome Rain Publishers) pp. vii-xiii.

Illustrations were provided by *The Picture Reference File, Volume II* (New York: Hart Publishing Company) and *ArtToday.com*.

Some limericks were based on jokes from re-runs of TV's *Laugh In, Geezer.com, BetterGolf.net,* and *The Vent* published in the Atlanta Journal-Constitution.